W9-BUM-647

0 00 30 0312296 1

Broken Bones

Dr. Alvin Silverstein,

Virginia Silverstein, and

Laura Silverstein Nunn

My Health

Franklin Watts

A Division of Grolier Publishing

New York • London • Hong Kong • Sydney

Danbury, Connecticut

Photographs©: Anatomyworks: 17 (Leonard Dank), 16 right (Lauren Shavell); Envision: 37 (Steven Needham); Liaison Agency, Inc.: 25 (Bruce Plotkin); Medichrome: 31 (M. English), 32 (Ken Lax); Peter Arnold Inc.: 35 (Zeva Oelbaum), 5; Photo Researchers, NY: 21 (Quest/SPL), 14 (David Gifford/SPL), 39 (Phillip Hayson), 30 (Dr. P. Marazzi/SPL), 11 left (Astrid & Hanns-Frieder Michler/SPL), 11 right (Alfred Pasieka/SPL), 27 (CNRI/SPL), 28 (MVI/SS), 7 (Catherine Ursillo); PhotoEdit: 33 (Richard Hutchings), 4, 16 left (David Young-Wolff); Stone: 36 (Gary Holscher), 12 (Yorgos Nikas), 19 (UHB Trust); Superstock, Inc.: 23; The Image Works: 20 (Ellen Senisi).

Cartoons by Rick Stromoski
Medical illustration by Leonard Morgan

Visit Franklin Watts on the Internet at:
http://publishing.grolier.com

Library of Congress Cataloging-in-Publication Data

Silverstein, Alvin.
 Broken bones / by Alvin Silverstein, Virginia Silverstein, and Laura Silverstein Nunn.
 p. cm.—(My health)
 Includes bibliographical references and index.
 ISBN 0-531-11781-2 (lib. bdg.) 0-531-13968-9 (pbk.)
 1. Fractures—Juvenile literature. 2. Bones—Wounds and injuries—Juvenile literature. [1. Fractures. 2. Bones—Wounds and injuries.] I. Silverstein, Virginia B. II. Nunn, Laura Silverstein. III. Title. IV. Series.

RD101 .S49 2001
617.1'5—dc21
 00-28208

GROLIER
PUBLISHING

Contents

Crack!

You just got some brand-new in-line skates, and you are trying them out for the first time. Just as you're starting to get the hang of them, you suddenly lose your balance. As you hit the ground, you hear a terrible cracking sound. Ouch! Your arm looks crooked, and it hurts so much you can't help crying. You have broken a bone.

All the bones in your body fit together to make up your **skeleton**. Your skeleton gives your body its shape. Your bones help you sit in a chair, walk across a room, jump up and down, pick up a

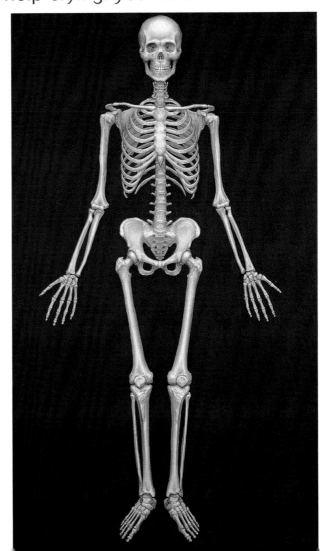

◀ This girl has lost her balance and is about to fall. Will she break an arm?

▶ The bones in your body form your skeleton. They help support all your inside parts.

5

book, and throw a ball. Every time you move, you use your bones. That's why bones are so important.

Bones are hard and tough, but they can break if you twist them the wrong way or something hits them really hard. You've probably had plenty of cuts and scrapes. They're no big deal. A broken bone is more serious—and more painful. If you ever think you might have a broken bone, you should go to the hospital right away.

Read on to find out how a doctor can treat a broken bone. You will also learn more about your amazing bones and how they repair themselves.

Did You Know...

More than 50 percent of all Americans will break a bone before they are 18 years old.

Inside Your Bones

Have you ever made a wish using a wishbone from a chicken or turkey? If you waited until the wishbone dried, it probably broke fairly easily as you pulled on it. Your bones are very different from breakable, dried-up wishbones or the stonelike dinosaur bones you see in a science museum.

Over millions of years, the bones of these dinosaurs became fossils.

Your bones are hard and strong because of the way they are made. Bones contain **minerals** that come from the foods you eat. These minerals are held together by a weblike network of **collagen** fibers. If the collagen were removed from your bones, they would

Activity 1:
Making a Model of a Bone

You can make a model that shows how minerals and collagen work together to make bones so strong. You will need two cardboard tubes (from paper towel or toilet paper rolls), masking tape, plaster of paris, a large spoon, water, an old bowl or bucket, and some cheesecloth.

Begin by placing masking tape over one end of an empty cardboard tube. Mix plaster of paris with water according to the instructions on the package. Use the spoon to fill the cardboard tube with plaster of paris. When the plaster is completely dry, peel off the cardboard mold. Now you have a long, solid piece of plaster that is shaped like a bone. It is firm and

crumble. If the minerals were removed, your bones would become rubbery. The minerals and collagen in your bones contain water that helps give bones their shape and strength. Bones also contain living cells—just like the rest of your body.

stiff, but it is not very strong. You can break it easily, just by bending it with your hands or knocking it against the edge of a table.

Place a roll of cheesecloth several layers of thick inside another cardboard tube, seal one end of the tube with tape, and fill that tube with plaster of paris. When the plaster sets, you will have another long, solid piece of plaster. It will look like the first one you made, but it will be harder to break this second "bone." The layers of cheesecloth inside make a big difference.

The hard, solid plaster gives your model its shape. The weblike network of cheesecloth fibers gives the model its strength. Without collagen fibers, bones would be weak and brittle—just like the plaster model without the cheesecloth.

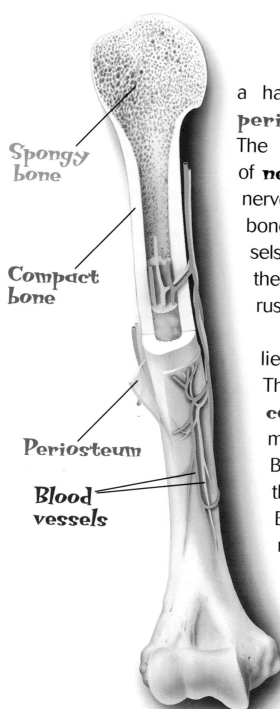

Spongy bone

Compact bone

Periosteum

Blood vessels

When you look at a bone, you see a hard, white covering called the **periosteum** (pehr-ee-OSS-tee-um). The periosteum contains a network of **nerves** and **blood vessels**. The nerves carry messages between your bones and your brain. The blood vessels bring important nutrients, such as the minerals calcium and phosphorus, to your bones.

The toughest part of your bone lies just below the periosteum. This smooth, hard layer is called **compact bone**. It is made up of minerals that are arranged in rings. Blood vessels and nerves pass through the center of each ring. Below the compact bone is a lacy network of bone. This layer is called **spongy bone** because it looks a lot like a sponge. It is almost as strong as compact bone, but it is much lighter because part of it is just empty space.

This is what compact
bone looks like when
it has been magnified
16,000 times. Blood
vessels that pass
through rings of bony
minerals nourish the
cells inside your bones. ▶

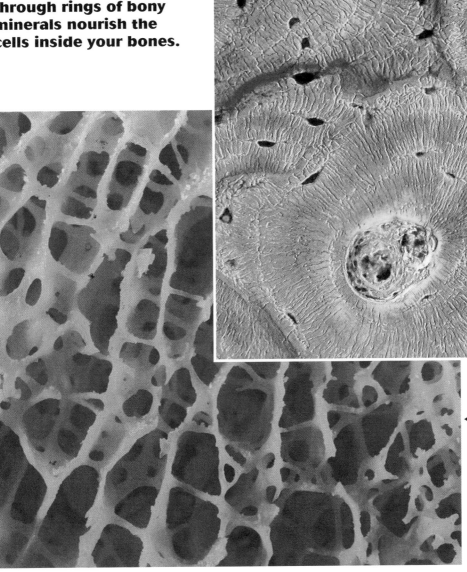

◀ This is a
close-up view
of spongy
bone. It may
look light
and airy, but
it's really
very strong.

The insides of the large bones in your body are partly hollow, like a tube. The space within them is filled with a jellylike substance called **bone marrow**. Bone marrow produces blood cells. Red blood cells carry oxygen through your blood to various parts of the body. White blood cells fight germs when you get a cut or the flu. Bone marrow also makes **platelets**. Platelets help you stop bleeding when you get a cut.

Red blood cells (center, red), white blood cells (right, yellow), and platelets (left) are all made inside your bone marrow. Here they are shown more than 600,000 times their true size.

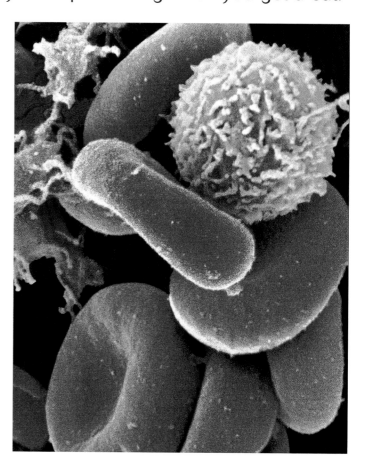

Why Do Broken Bones Hurt?

When you cut your finger or bang your knee, nerves send messages to your brain that let you feel pain. There are no pain nerves inside your bones, so why does a broken bone hurt so much? Actually, it's not really the bone that hurts. When a bone cracks or breaks, the periosteum is also damaged. Nerves in the periosteum send lots of pain messages up to the brain, and you feel pain.

As you can see, your bones help your body in many important ways. They make blood cells and platelets. They also give your body its shape and make it possible for you to lift a glass of milk or run across a field.

How Do Bones Move?

Your bones can't move all by themselves. They need some help. Bones are connected to one another at **joints**. The bones at some joints, such as those in the skull, do not move. These joints are called fixed joints. Most of the joints in your body are moving joints. There are two main types— hinge joints and ball-and-socket joints. Hinge joints are found in your elbows and knees. They move in only one direction, like a door hinge.

Ball-and-socket joints can move in any direction. To see what a ball-and-socket

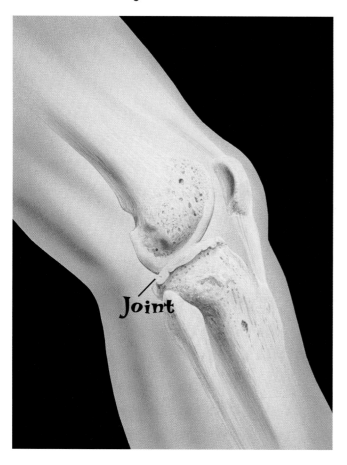

Joint

The leg bones are joined at the knee in a hinge joint.

14

joint looks like, make a fist with one hand. Now cup the fingers of your other hand around it. This is what a ball-and-socket joint looks like. You can turn your fist (the ball) freely in any direction within the socket formed by your other hand. The joints at your shoulders and hips are ball-and-socket joints.

If the bones that fit together in a joint were actually touching one another, they would rub and scrape every time you move. The ends of the bones would get hot, and they would wear away. Fortunately, the end of each bone is covered with a cushion of tough, rubbery **cartilage**. This is the gristle you find at the end of chicken bones. These moving joints are also "oiled" with a special liquid that helps them move smoothly.

Bones can't move without **muscles**. Your muscles work your bones like strings work a puppet. When a puppeteer pulls on the puppet's strings, the puppet can walk and dance. When muscles pull on your bones, you can move.

Muscles can only pull on bones. They cannot push. When you bend your arm to "make a muscle,"

BUCKET 'O' CHICKEN PARTS

the big muscle on the inside of your upper arm tightens. The fibers that make up the muscle get shorter and pull on the bones in your forearm. When you straighten your arm, these muscle fibers relax and stretch out again. At the same time, a different muscle, on the outside of your upper arm, tightens and its fibers shorten. The bones in your forearm are pulled out straight again. Muscles generally work in pairs.

Muscles are attached to bones by tough cords called **tendons**. These tendons do not stretch or

When you bend your arm up, the biceps muscle bulges as it pulls on the bone in the forearm.

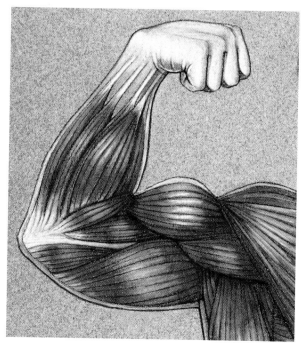

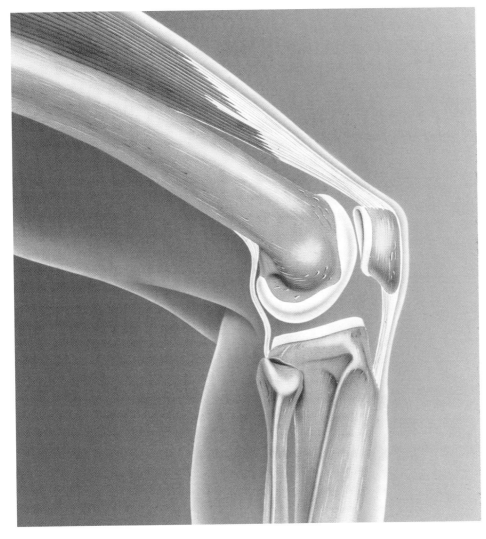

A tough tendon (white) holds your kneecap in place and connects your thigh muscle (red) to your tibia—one of the bones in your lower leg.

shorten the way muscles do. Many muscles are narrow at both ends where they meet the tendons. Look at the back of your hand while you move your fingers up and down. As you lift your fingers, you can see the tendons that connect your finger bones to your wrist.

Snap, Crackle, and Pop

It sounds like you're breaking bones when you "crack your knuckles." Actually, the snapping sound may be the popping of air bubbles in the fluid inside the joints. Or it may be caused by ligaments that are stretched out tight like guitar strings as they slide across the knuckle bones. Either way, it doesn't hurt.

Bones are fastened to other bones by *ligaments*. Ligaments are strong straps that wrap around joints to hold bones together. They can stretch more than tendons, so they allow bones to move freely without coming apart. Ligaments keep your joints from slipping out of place. They hold the arm bones in place in the shoulder joints and help to keep your knees steady. Ligaments also hold many small bones together in the ankles and wrists.

Bones for a Lifetime

Your bones are constantly changing throughout your life. All those changes started before you were even born. While you were still developing inside your mother's body, you already had a complete skeleton. That skeleton was not made of bone. It was made of soft, rubbery cartilage. Little by little the cartilage was replaced by bone.

You grew very quickly before you were born. After birth, you continued to grow rapidly. As you grew, bone continued to fill in the cartilage "model" of your skeleton. The hard bone added support, so you were soon able to hold your head up, sit, stand, and walk.

Growing Up

Girls usually have their growth spurt about 2 years earlier than boys. That's why many girls are taller than boys their age for a couple of years. Eventually, the boys will catch up—and then they grow taller than the girls. Most girls reach their full height in their mid-teens. Boys usually reach their full height in their late teens.

These two kids are both 10 years old. The girl is taller now, but that will probably change in a few years.

All this time, your bones were growing along with the rest of your body—and they are still growing. In a few years, when you go through **puberty**, your bones will go through a big "growth spurt." In just a few months, you will grow several inches taller. Your bones will keep on growing until your middle or late teens, when you have reached your full height.

By the time you are 25 years old, your bones will be hard and strong, but the cartilage in your nose and ears will remain as cartilage for your whole life.

Even after you finish growing, your bones can still change. Like a sculptor molding clay, bones can be remodeled. Bones become thicker when a load is placed on them. Your bones will get stronger and thicker when you lift heavy objects or exercise, even after you are an adult. If you don't get enough exercise, your bones can get thinner and break more easily.

Why does this happen? Special cells inside your bones help them grow, repair damaged tissue, and lay down calcium deposits to make the bones hard. The bone-building cells that make new bone tissue are called *osteoblasts*, which means "bone formers."

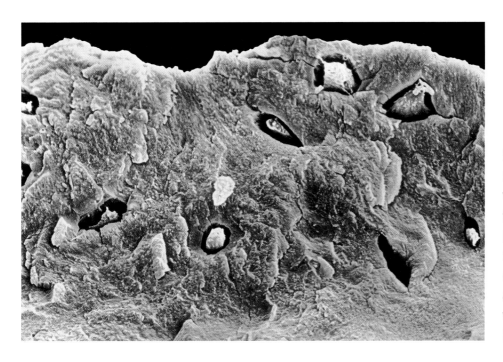

In this magnified view taken through a powerful microscope, osteoblasts are hard at work building bone.

You have more bones than your mother or father. Each of your parents has 206 bones, but you have dozens more. Bones do not disappear as you grow older—some of them grow together. A newborn baby has more than 300 bones!

Me =206
Baby= 300+

Another kind of bone cell also plays an important part in the growth of bones. These cells are called **osteoclasts**, which means "bone breakers."

Osteoclasts and osteoblasts work together to keep your bones healthy. Osteoclasts eat away small parts of bones. This releases calcium, phosphate, and other minerals into the body. The osteoblasts fill in the areas of missing bone with layers of collagen. Calcium and other minerals are added to the crisscrossing layers of collagen fibers to create new, hard bone.

This process will continue until you are about 35 years old. Then it starts to slow down, and the bones start to become thin and weak. That's one reason why older people are more likely to break a bone in a fall than you are.

When Bones Break

It's really not that easy to break a bone. Think about how many times you fell down on a patch of ice. What about all those times you jumped off a swing or fell off your bicycle? You probably got a few scrapes or maybe a big black-and-blue mark, but a broken bone? Probably not.

Bones *can* break though. If something hits your bone really hard or a joint is bent too far the wrong way, that bone may crack or snap. A broken bone is called a **fracture**. Bones can be broken in different ways, so doctors use different names for different kinds of fractures.

It's easy to fall when you're ice skating, but you probably won't break a bone.

All About Fractures

Kinds of Fractures	What Happens
Simple or closed fracture	The bone breaks but does not stick out through the skin. (Most fractures are simple.)
Compound or open fracture	The broken bone pierces through the skin. This can be serious because germs can enter the skin and cause an **infection**.
Incomplete or greenstick fracture	The bone cracks and bends but does not break completely. Young children are most likely to have this kind of fracture.
Impact fracture	The broken ends of the bone are jammed together by the force of the accident.
Comminuted fracture	The bone shatters into many pieces.
Single, double, or multiple fracture	One, two, or many breaks in the same bone

Kids who are active and play sports are more likely to break a bone than someone who spends a lot of time reading, playing on the computer, or watching TV. But you never know when an accident might happen. You could break an arm when you trip over a toy lying on your bedroom floor or slip in the bathtub.

This boy broke his arm while riding on a skate-board, but there are lots of other ways to break a bone.

The moment you break a bone, your body starts working hard to fix the problem. When platelets come across a damaged blood vessel, they become sticky. They catch on the rough edges of the torn blood vessel or broken bone and stick there. Soon more and more platelets arrive at the scene. Some break open and spill out chemicals that start a chain of reactions in the blood. These reactions produce sticky fibers, which form a mesh that traps red blood cells.

Within minutes, a large blood **clot** has formed. The clot hardens around the broken ends of your bone and fills in the gap between them. This clot becomes a framework for the cells that form new bone and eventually heal the fracture.

Meanwhile, broken blood vessels in and around the bone spill fluid out into the surrounding tissues. The tissues swell up and become **inflamed**. The skin above the wound turns red and feels hot and painful.

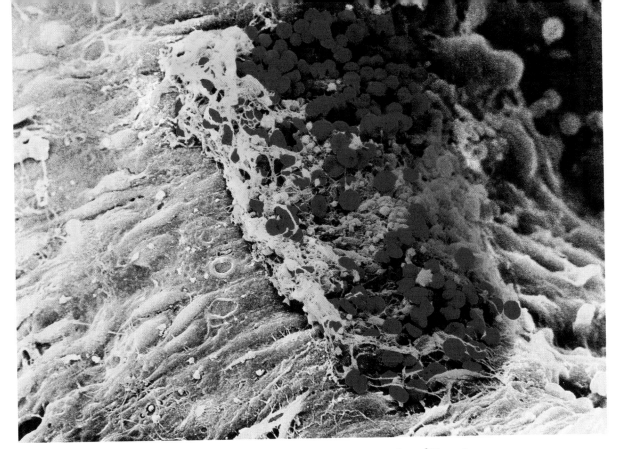

When you break a bone, platelets break open and spill out chemicals. Soon a network of sticky fibers (orange) starts to form a blood clot that traps red blood cells (red).

The damaged blood vessels also release chemicals that send out signals. They call in the clean-up squad—the white blood cells. White blood cells are jelly-like blobs that can swim through the blood and can even squeeze through the spaces between body cells. White cell clean-up squads gobble up dead cells and any germs or bits of dirt that have entered the wound.

Once the white blood cells are finished, your bone cells go to work. When a bone breaks, the part of the bone around the broken edges dies. As minerals seep out, the ends of the bone become soft. Bone-breaking osteoclasts eat away the soft, dead part of the bone. Then osteoblasts come in and lay down a new network of collagen. This forms a bridge between the broken ends of your bone. Finally, calcium and other minerals are added to the collagen to repair the break. This new area of bone is called a **callus**.

Repairing a bone takes a long time. Bone cells remove dead parts of the bone and then lay down new material. This process forms a callus. Eventually the "rough patch" is reshaped and the rebuilt area looks just like it did before the break.

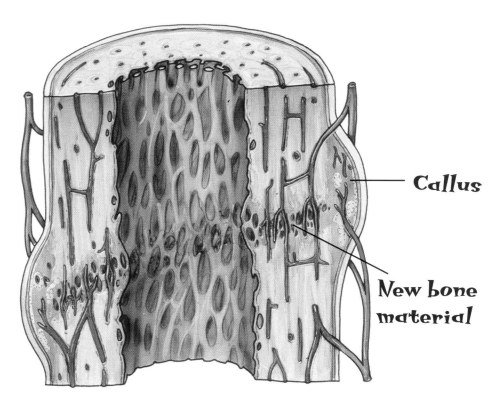

Callus

New bone material

After the callus forms, the bone-breaking cells come back to finish the job. They eat away at the outside of the bridge, shaping it to look like the original bone. Gradually, the callus hardens to form true bone.

When the callus is completely hardened, the bone is as strong as it was before you broke it. In fact, a doctor looking at an **X ray** of a fully healed broken bone may not be able to tell where the break was.

Although your body works hard to heal your bones, they often need special medical attention to heal properly. The two broken ends have to be lined up just right. Otherwise, the bones may look crooked when they heal.

Did You Know....

Kids are fast healers. A wrist fracture in an adult may take up to 8 weeks to heal. In a five-year-old, the same break may heal in only 3 weeks.

SMTWTFS

What the Doctor Does

How can you tell if you have broken a bone? There are some telltale signs. Sometimes you can hear a bone break. Other times you can see that a bone or joint is not shaped right. You may even see a broken bone sticking out through your skin. You may also have a broken bone if a joint—such as the elbow or knee—looks swollen, and you can't move it.

It's easy to see that this finger is broken, but not all broken bones are so obvious.

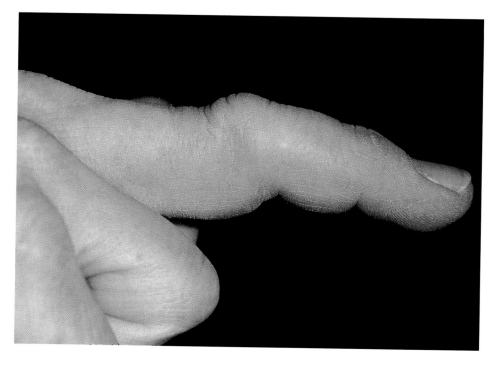

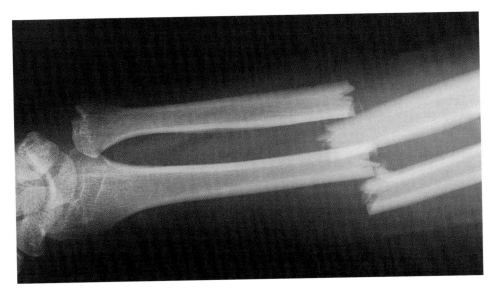

Ouch! This X ray clearly shows that both of the bones in this person's lower arm are broken.

If you think you have a fracture, don't move! When a bone is broken, the surrounding muscles, joints, and ligaments are also affected. If you move a broken bone, you might make the damage even worse.

Ask someone to help make a **splint** to keep the fractured bone from moving. Almost anything can be used to make a splint—a thin piece of wood, plastic, a rolled-up magazine, or even an umbrella. Use some string or tape to strap the splint to the injured area.

The doctor needs to take an X ray to see whether the bone is broken and how serious the damage is. If the bone has been knocked out of place, the doctor will have to line it up just right so that it can heal properly.

If you have a simple fracture, the doctor can probably force the broken ends back into place with his or her hands. This could be really painful, but the doctor can give you medicine to relieve the pain.

For more serious fractures, the doctor may need to do surgery to put the bones back into the right position. Sometimes doctors put pins inside your body to keep the broken parts from moving after they are lined up. After the bone is healed, the doctor may remove the pins.

Once the bone is set, you will then be fitted with a **cast** to keep the broken bone from moving while it is healing. A cast may be made from plaster of paris, fiberglass, or plastic. Plaster casts can be molded to fit the shape of your body, but they are heavy and bulky. Also, you cannot get a plaster cast wet. If you do, it may soften and crumble. Fiberglass casts are

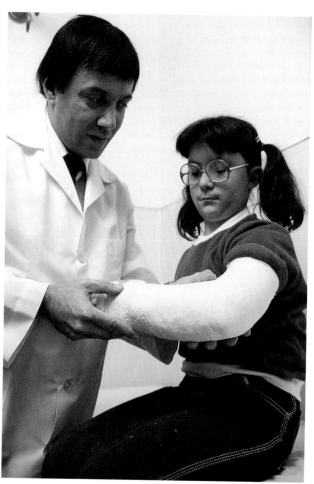

A plaster cast keeps a broken bone in place until it heals.

much lighter and you can get them wet, but they do not fit as closely over a fracture as a plaster cast does.

You may have to wear a cast for up to 3 months. When the bone has healed, the doctor will cut the cast off. If you have been wearing a hard plaster cast, the doctor will use a noisy saw with a round, dull blade. Don't worry, even if the blade touches your skin, it won't hurt. In fact, it might even tickle.

Scientists are always looking for new ways to help broken bones heal faster. Doctors can now use a special

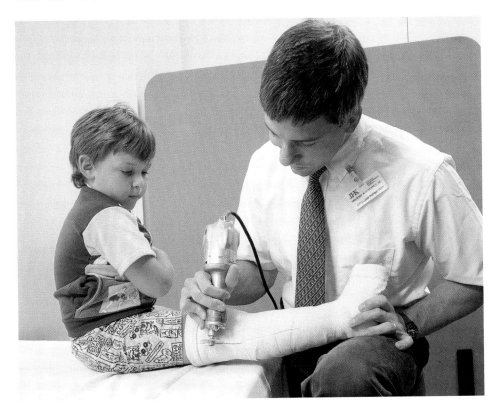

A doctor removes a child's cast.

kind of glue to repair a simple wrist fracture. This glue, which looks like toothpaste, contains calcium and phosphorus. It holds the broken wrist bones together while they heal. Osteoclasts eat their way through the hardened paste just as they eat through bone. Then osteoblasts arrive and build strong new bone to repair the break. A patient with a broken wrist usually has to wear a cast for 6 to 8 weeks. When doctors use the

Smaller and Weaker

If you have a broken arm or leg, you may notice something surprising when the doctor removes the cast. The arm or leg might seem smaller and weaker than it used to be. You might have trouble throwing a ball or walking across a room.

When you don't use your muscles and bones for a long time, they **atrophy**. They get thinner and weaker. You will need to exercise the weakened body part to get your strength back. The doctor may suggest that you see a **physical therapist**.

glue, the cast can be replaced by a removable splint after only 2 weeks.

Doctors may also apply **ultrasound waves** or a small electrical charge to the broken area. You won't feel a thing, but your bones will heal twice as fast and there will be less muscle damage.

Even with all these new techniques, waiting for a broken bone to heal can take a lot of patience. So the best thing to do is avoid breaking them in the first place.

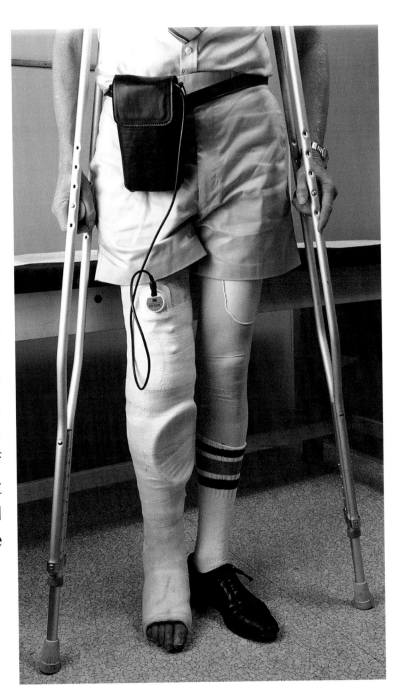

This high-tech cast includes an electrical device that will speed up the healing process.

Take Care of Your Bones

When you are active—at school, at home, or around the neighborhood there are things you can do to protect yourself.

When you ride a bike, ice skate, in-line skates, or play sports, be sure to wear protective gear. A bicycle helmet or knee and wrist pads can prevent broken bones. Don't be a daredevil when you play on swings or a jungle gym. Your bones may be strong, but why take chances on a bad break?

You can also avoid accidents at home. Don't leave clothes, toys, and games on the floor. Before you rush down the stairs, think about what might happen.

It's cool to play it safe! You should always wear protective gear.

There are also things you can do to keep your bones healthy. Getting enough sleep is important for your body's growth and repair. Regular exercise is important, too. The more stress you put on bones, the more they will grow. When you move your bones a lot and force them to support weight, they get thicker and stronger.

You should also try to eat a variety of foods. A balanced diet includes plenty of fruit, vegetables, breads, cereals, and pasta as well as some meats and dairy products. It's OK to eat candy and cookies some-times, but you shouldn't eat too much junk food. These foods contain a lot of sugars and fats. They can make you feel tired and cranky.

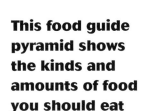

This food guide pyramid shows the kinds and amounts of food you should eat every day.

Activity 2:
Testing for Fats

How can you tell whether a food contains a lot of fat? Try the following test on a variety of foods. You might also want to include butter, hamburger, French fries or potato chips, carrots, milk, and apple juice.

Cut several 3-inch (7-cm) squares out of a brown paper bag and label each of the foods you are testing. If the food is a solid, rub some of it onto the square. If the food is a liquid, put a few drops of it on the square. Let the squares dry and then hold each square up to the light. If the light shines through the square, the food contains a lot of fat.

While you are still growing, it is important to eat meat and other foods with a lot of protein. Proteins provide the basic building blocks for new tissues. Vitamins and minerals are important too.

As you grow taller, your bones are growing larger. You need a new supply of calcium and phosphorus each day to build strong bones. You can get these minerals by drinking milk, and eating cheeses, yogurt, and green, leafy vegetables.

For minerals to do their job, you also need to get enough vitamin D. Vitamin D helps your body absorb calcium and phosphorus from your food. This important vitamin forms when cells in your skin are exposed to sunlight. It is also added to milk and dairy products.

If you eat a lot of chips and soda and avoid foods with calcium and protein, your bones will not be strong and healthy. Weak, brittle bones are much more likely to break when you fall. If you take good care of your bones, they will take care of you.

Milk helps keep your bones healthy. It contains calcium, phosphorus, and vitamin D.

Glossary

atrophy—a shrinking and weakening of a body part or tissue that occurs when it is not used

blood vessel—one of the tubes that carries blood throughout the body

bone marrow—the jellylike substance found inside large bones. Red blood cells, white blood cells, and platelets form in bone marrow.

callus—a new growth of bone joining the broken ends of a fracture

cartilage—the tough, stretchy tissue at the ends of bones in adults. Cartilage makes up most of the skeleton in young children.

cast—a hard covering made of plaster or plastic. It is used to hold a fracture in place while it heals.

clot—a jellylike solid formed by blood to close up a wound

collagen—a tough protein fiber that holds bones together and helps make them strong

compact bone—the hard layer of a bone with minerals arranged in rings. It contains blood vessels that nourish the bones.

fracture—a broken bone

infection—when the body is invaded by germs that multiply and damage tissues

inflamed—red, hot, and swollen tissues that have been damaged

joint—a kind of body tissue that forms between bones

ligament—a tough band of tissue that wraps around joints and holds bones together

mineral—a chemical that comes from the foods you eat and is used to build blood cells, bones, and teeth. Calcium, phosphorus, and iron are minerals.

muscle—a strong, elastic tissue that pulls on bones or other structures and moves body parts

nerve—a structure the carries messages to and from the brain

osteoblast—a bone-building cell that makes new bone tissue

osteoclast—a bone cell that breaks up old bone tissue

periosteum—the outer layer of a bone

physical therapist—a health-care professional who helps patients learn how to use damaged body parts

platelets—tiny blood particles that help to stop bleeding when the body is injured

puberty—a process in which a child goes through physical changes and becomes an adult

skeleton—the bony framework that supports the body and gives it shape

splint—a thin piece of wood or some other material used to keep a fractured bone from moving

spongy bone—the light airy inside part of a bone that looks a lot like a sponge

tendon—a tough band of tissue that connects a muscle to a bone

ultrasound waves—sound waves that are too high-pitched for people to hear

X ray—a picture used to see the bones and other internal body structures

Learning More

Books

Anderson, Karen C. and Stephen Cumbaa. *The Bones and Skeleton Game Book: A Challenging Collection of Puzzles and Projects*. New York: Workman, 1993.

Black, Sonia W. *All About My Skeleton Activity Book*. New York: Scholastic, Inc., 1994.

Gross, Ruth Belov. *A Book About Your Skeleton*. New York: Scholastic Inc., 1994.

Sandeman, Anna. *Bones*. Brookfield, CT: Copper Beech Books, 1995.

Weitzman, Elizabeth. *Let's Talk About: Having a Broken Bone*. New York: Rosen, 1997.

Organizations and Online Sites

Broken Bones
http://www.kidshealth.org/parent/healthy/broken_bones.html
This site describes what happens when kids break bones and how their bones heal.

Broken Bones

http://www.healthy.net/library/Books/Healthyself/broken-bones.htm

This site is maintained by the American Institute of Preventive Medicine. It has general information about bones as well as tips for avoiding injuries. It also explains what to do if you break a bone.

Broken Bones

http://KidsHealth.org/cgi-bin/wais/search.pl?broken+bones

This site features lots of easy-to-read information and a long list of links on broken bones.

New Ways to Heal Broken Bones

http://www.fda.gov/fdac/features/396_bone.html

This article from *FDA Consumer Magazine* includes information about how bones grow and describes ways to heal them when they break.

Why Do Broken Bones Hurt?

http://www.nursing.uiowa.edu/sites/pedspain/GenePain/Brokennt.htm

This article provides easy-to-understand information about broken bones and why they hurt.

Index

Page numbers in *italics* indicate illustrations.

About the Authors

Dr. Alvin Silverstein is a professor of biology at the College of Staten Island of the City University of New York. **Virginia B. Silverstein** is a translator of Russian scientific literature. The Silversteins first worked together on a research project at the University of Pennsylvania. Since then, they have produced 6 children and more than 160 published books for young people.

    Laura Silverstein Nunn, a graduate of Kean College, has been helping with her parents' books since her high-school days. She is the coauthor of more than thirty books on diseases and health, science concepts, endangered species, and pets. Laura lives with her husband Matt and their young son Cory in a rural New Jersey town not far from her childhood home.